Poetically Divorced In The Raw

Poetically Divorced In The Raw

Harold A. Boreanaz

HAB-Z Publishing
Waterbury, Vermont

HAB-Z Publishing
PO Box 125
Waterbury, Vermont

© 2019 Harold A. Boreanaz

Cover and Illustrations © 2019 Elijah Werth

All Rights Reserved

ISBN 978-1-7339505-0-3

Bulk copies can be ordered from the publisher at the above address.

Raw write it will be alright.
Just let it flow right
      into the show
Shoot from the hip
      don't care what you hit.
Don't read it back
      this is not an act.
Sometimes despair is all you need
So write it down and you will succeed.
Raw write is the right write.

You own the key to my heart,
It's been yours from the start.
I can't find another at Walmart.
There's nothing in my shopping cart.
No space for me on the love chart.
Ever since you decided to part,
   been standing in a gallery without any art.

Born first of five in Buffalo, New York. Moved to Vermont following my sister, Lynn's footsteps.

I brought my young daughter to Vermont to get away from the city. The pollution, the crime, the congestion, and yes, sorry to say, the ex. It was the situation I thought was best for my daughter and myself.

I was introduced to my second wife by my sister. I can't say what happened, but I will say that it was her. Never thought I would get over our D-Day. But then through mutual friends of my sister and my brother-in-law's pointing her out in a canoe on a mountain lake, I met the "love of my life."

Now you are up-to-date so I'm exiting broken-hearted and so shattered but

                        Poetically,

                        Harold A. Boreanaz

One of the saddest days of my life was the day my love light walked out of my world. There have been a few losses in my time but this one is right up there.

In an attempt to hold on to my soulmate/girlfriend of 15 years, I bought 50 flameless candles and set them up all around my bedroom. What a sight like something in a movie. I can't have regular candles in my apartment/ fire regulations. (Now what the hell am I going to do with 50 candles that need batteries?) Well, she stayed the night with me in my bed. (It took a while for both of us to get up the courage, but then everything went fine in bed like always!)

It's out of bed she has a problem with. She said she wants to be free. She doesn't want to have a relationship with me anymore. And she's moving to North Carolina. That's when the floor really came out from under me. After some cerebral surreal shock time, I walked her out the door, we kissed, held each other for a moment, and she drove away with a wave and a blown kiss into the sunset (even though it was 9.30 a.m.).

Life will never be the same again without her. "Now I'm down almost level with the ground." "I'm so low I have to look up to see the grass."

"I have Rock & Roll in my soul, can't help it. Can you tell?"

It's really hard listening to music by myself now that you have gone. It makes me cry too much. That's quite a shame because I *really* like listening to music by myself *very* loud. Now I can't for very long depending on the song.

And when people are around, I have to turn away from them and try and hold back. Sometimes I can't. Then I have to leave the area and swear out loud to shake it off. Sometimes I am consumed with emotion while I'm working and it slows me down. And the tears in my eyes dripping on my glasses is not good for business. I can't keep crying like this. How could you have not known it would go this way. I never had a chance. You know how much you mean to me. I need you to help me understand why you kept this from me for so long and to wait until it was too late to change things. People can change for someone they care for with all their heart. You seem to want all your changes to be for yourself to decide and carry out.

What about your partner (significant other)? Just how significant was I (am I)? I guess not enough. I know, as much as I wish these words could, they are not getting you back anytime soon, if ever, but they are significant to me. So please tell me what level of significance I fell under on your list of significants.

Because you are and always will be at the top of my list.

P. S. I haven't even touched any of my monopoly game pieces. They are sitting on my table. What is the point of winning a million of anything when you lost the one that means everything!

If there was even a tiny chance we could get back together, somewhere down the line, I would never go to Ontario if it might be a deal breaker for you because I'm not that kind of guy anyway.

Please stay in touch. Please stay friends. I'll try to back off a little but it's only been a couple of days and shock wave hasn't settled yet.

The Love of My Life Does Not Want to be My Wife

The love of my life does not want to be my wife
Now she is gone and moved far away.
I miss her more each passing day.
She said she still has some things to do.
I'm feeling the depth of the ocean's deepest blue.
I never knew love could hurt like this.
Remembering that day we had our last kiss.
My world has stopped turning and I have fallen from grace.
Knowing I might never get to see her face.
I gave her my all, I was her biggest fan.
She went and threw my heart in the garbage can.
So I'm like the tin man with the empty space in his chest.
Not lying beside her I can't take my rest.
Sunglasses pulled tight with tears in my eyes.
The look on my face I cannot disguise.

Anytime I Cry

Sometimes don't know why
But when I think of you
That's when it is my cue
Tears come pouring out
I just want to shout
I can't touch your face
My world's gone to waste
Darling what will I do?
No more lovin' days with you
I should carry on and move along
But I just haven't finished the song
As I sit here with this pain
It's so easy to explain
So don't ask me to try
Anytime I cry
Anytime I cry
I sure know why
It will turn glad to sad
It will make/drive you mad
The only girl for me
Is moving to the sea.
I'm in an ocean of pain
And I can't pull the drain
So now you know why
Anytime I cry

After many years of life I've found a way to help stop crying. Now this is for myself. Do not try this for yourself.

What I do if I can't control crying within, I just swear out loud a few times and it helps me stop. Now this presents a problem in public places.

So instead of looking hysterically sad, I look like a rude loud mouth. So now I just put on a little act and people leave me alone.

And I wrote a little song about my problem and it goes like this:

My Tourette's Girl

As I watched you slowly walk out my door
Knowing you don't want my love anymore.
It didn't take long to really sink in.
I'm hurting so bad right under my skin
Feels like my heart is broken in two
I only own half the other is for you
F………..   F………...   S………...   S……………

We know pain brings joy and joy brings pain
These feelings right now I cannot explain.
See, you never really gave me a chance.
I guess I'm a victim of circumstance.
Now I can't look at your sweet smiling face
This truly will be my biggest disgrace.
F………..   F………...   S………...   S……………

I might make it through but not unscathed
I'm not in control of how I behave.
The power of love is stronger than us.
That's why I feel like I was hit by a bus.
F………..   F………...   S………...   S……………

Just about anytime I hear your name
I get Tourette's syndrome much to my shame
Swearing in public I just shouldn't do.
It just sort of happens when I'm thinking of you.
F………..   F………...   S………...   S……………
I don't think it's helping me get over you.

I took out some lines that I first wrote to fit the rhyme. But I didn't feel it that way towards (her) whom I still love very much. The lines went at the end of the third verse and went like this: If I ever see you in this lifetime, I don't think I'd even loan you a dime. Clever, but I didn't mean it towards her.

Lost

Lost in the woods never to be found
Lost in space cause I can't see your face.
Lost in love's canyon far below the ground
Lost in the memories of your beauty and grace
Lost in a dark cave and I can't hear a sound
Lost in a dream where I'm back in your place.
Lost in a world without you around.
Lost in a game not even holding an ace.
Lost in a time when our souls were bound
Lost in your arms if I had my case
Lost under a weight feels like a thousand pounds
Lost in an ocean of tears so deep I may drown
Lost the love of my life I'm a big disgrace
Lost the light in my life you can see it on my face
Lost into the night now I can't be found
Lost in love's whirlpool going round and round

So How Do I Feel?

Trying to contain the intense pain of being
Hit by a train takes a lot of restrain
I'll try to explain but probably in vain
Cause I have a railroad spike in my brain

Heart Pen and Paper

As I write down this song thinking of you
How it will turn out I haven't a clue.
From my heart to my pen to my paper
She's got a grip on my soul can't escape her.
Now she's out of reach and gone to the beach
Oh, what will I do I'm really so blue.
I'll golf on the turf and learn how to surf
If that could help me get back to you.
You've left me before you say this is the last
Both my body and soul are in a hardened cast

From my heart to my pen to my paper
Can't escape her.
Can't escape how I feel
Can't escape from your gaze
Can't escape this big deal
Can't escape memories of days
Can't escape in a world of purple haze

From my heart to my pen to my paper
Can't escape her

Two Was One But One Made It Two

You really never gave me the key to your car
    your home or your heart.
That always gave me the feeling we would one day part.
It makes me sadder every day,
Not much anyone could say,
I thought the love we had was a work of art.
Anytime I start to think of you,
I stop all it is I'm supposed to do
Tears get in my way,
Can't see the light of day,
One and one was one but now it's two.
So if you ever change your mind,
Just look for me I'm an easy find,
I'm just hanging on the wall,
Waiting for your call,
In this picture frame with you on my mind.

I really thought and really do want us to be together forever

Talking Through a Fan

It's like I'm "talking through a fan" pointed straight at you
What it is I am saying you haven't a clue
I hear words zooming out of my mouth not meaning a thing
"This is one love bite that really has a sting."
So if you listen close to my garbled voice
   you'll hear "My darling, you're my only choice"
I keep yelling in this fan as words flow through the air
Over and over again "For you is all I care"
Afraid to wake up without you afraid to go to sleep
Lying here alone all I can do is weep
As I'm walking through this world "without your hand in mine"
Even when I see it "I just can't feel the sunshine."
There's been a lot of hot air blowing through this fan
And I know some of it landed under the frying pan.
But some will float high endlessly through the air
If those words could grant a wish,
"Again into your eyes I'll stare!"

The Fall

If I leap from this ledge and fall through the sky
With your arms waiting for me, I would surely not die.
But if you were not there as I fell further down
They say you really never get to see the ground.
As I look out into an open abyss
To fall back to you is my only wish.
Now I'm hurling towards the earth.
Wondering what our love was worth.
Hope there's water down below.
It might be a better way to go.
You know these words are a figure of speech.
My love for you is never out of reach.
So if you really don't want our love anymore
I guess I can just plan on landing on the floor.

To the Love of My Life

Today is the day that love comes to town.
It's in the air but you can't hear a sound.
If you open your heart and let it in.
You will learn what you are about to win.
When past loves have brought you sadness and doubt.
This new love will make you stand up and shout.
So hold on tight and try not to look back.
The rewards of this joy you will not lack.
In darkness of night and the light of day.
The stars of your soul will lead you my way.
These are just words and they all say to you.
Our love is so strong that it must be true.
Love is as endless as the sands of time.
That's how I know ours will be just fine.
Sometimes love is hard and we all make mistakes.
But something like this you just can't fake.
Hold on to my hand and enjoy the ride.
Our love for each other we just can't hide.
So let's keep this going year after year.
Staying together will conquer all fear.
We are just human with faults of our own.
Love tells us all there is more to be shown.
So when we look back and we're old and gray,
Try to remember this Valentine's Day.
Try to remember the love on this day.
Our love is still what it was yesterday.

On a Cloud

I'm not gonna mention it too loud
But you really put me on a cloud
Doesn't take much to get me involved
Now you got a hold of my resolve
I'm in so deep can't seem to explain
Upon me now like a big freight train
Couldn't stop now even if I tried
Something like this you just cannot hide
The days begin and the days pass by
To spend them without you makes me sigh.
Though we're together often but brief
Every time we part it feels like grief.
Now I'm out here sitting on this wall
Without this love I would surely fall.
I know you're really not far away
It's just you're not here today
For when I wake up in the morning
It comes on me without a warning
Too far from you it's like a heavy shroud
But in your arms I'm back on that cloud
There are many ways to hide the pain
My tears for you I cannot refrain
Until we are close I will not rest
These things I have to get off my chest
This doesn't mean I'm down and out
I'll see you again there is no doubt
First time we met it was in a crowd
From that moment I was on that cloud
Looking down from way up here is great
Being up there with you I just can't wait
Counting the days till I can see you
Sitting here alone I have no clue
The times I talk to you on the phone
They help me to know that I'm not alone
Some things in life are not allowed.
I think I'll just stay here on this cloud.

Your Sweet Smiling Face

When the sky is dark and full of rain
I reach for you to open up the drain
If you're not with me now that's okay
You're still gonna brighten up my day
But when I see your sweet smiling face
The bad weather really has no place
If you want to come along with me
On a ship of love across the sea
To a place we've never been before
Take my hand and walk right through the door
There is no fear when we are together
So let's cast off into the weather
The ocean of love is deep and wide
There is no reason for us to hide
So show me your feelings every day
Togetherness is the only way.
When we're apart the world turns dark blue
It seems like there is nothing left to do
But when I see your sweet smiling face
The darkness leaves me without a trace
So if you're feeling a little gray
Turn to me and I will lead the way.
When you're alone hope you're thinking of me
Cause in your arms is where I want to be
When I'm alone looking into space
I can still see your sweet smiling face.

Socks

I laid my socks up against the wall.
Just been sitting here waiting for your call.
Anytime that phone starts to ring
I get ready to jump and sing!
If it's not you then that's okay.
I'll have to wait another day.
I know I'll hear from you some day.
When I'm awake that's all I pray.
Truly how much can one heart take?

Only you can make my earth shake
I know my radar is loud and clear
That's how I know you are not here.
But if you come in close enough
I will give you all the right stuff.
But time goes by, it ticks, it tocks
I think it's time to wash my socks
I'll wash my socks in hot or cold
My love for you will not get old.
I'll wash my socks if I so choose
So what do I have to lose
And until I get your call
Might not wash them at all
There's one thing that I know
Should never have let you go
Know I should buy another pair
But now I just don't really care
So until I receive that call
Those socks will stay against that wall
And the socks sang "When – Will – I – Be – Washed - - - - -"

That Merry Go Round Called Love

Feels like I'm in the Lost and Found
Love is like a merry-go-round
You're in or out never know when
Can it be now or was it then?

To ride the wheel or get off now
Just don't think I really know how.
Like to stay still for a minute
When you're on you're really in it.

But when you're off it turns real slow
That doesn't mean it's time to go.
The hope it will come back around
Will keep your feet right off the ground
So if you want to ride along
Hold on tight and sing your own song
Now I can hear your melody
I hope that tune is just for me.

If you're not lost you can't be found
Let's stay on this merry go round.
Around and round holding hands
Up and down across the lands
Wheel of love is always there.

It only works if you share.
Turning slow or turning fast
Get on board this ride's a blast
If you're lost or if you're found
Can't get off That merry go round
Don't – won't – stay right on.

Looking High

Looking high as any eye can see.
Looking higher than you and me.
Looking high in this bright room
Looking low into the dark gloom.
Looking high upon that hill.
Looking down on your own swill.
Looking down it will test your will
Looking down past the bar and grill
Looking down on the road kill.
Looking low into the dark of the night.
Looking low beyond your true fright.
Looking low down to your feet.
Looking low but won't be beat.
Looking high into the sky.
Looking high until you die.
Looking high is up not down.
Looking high won't let you drown.
Looking high every day and night
Looking high never stop the fight.

Mind Wash Nobody's Choice but Yours

What I have and could even
Imagine washing off my hands.
Pales in comparison, to what's on my mind.

You can wash your hands you can
Wash your face, you can wash
Them until there is no trace.

But the mind will always hold
That special place.

Trying to clean up what's going on out there.
Will not even compare to what's gonna go on here.

So wash your hands and wash your face
You can even try to clean up space.
But the mind is not meant to wash
Not in any race.

Sparkling clean and you think you're done
That's when you know you've just begun.
If you had your mother's hands and your mother's face
Would you even think of this disgrace?
So the mind is a terrible thing to wash

Clean is dirty, dirty is clean
I think you know just what I mean.

But the thoughts of your brain
While you're writing a song
Has nothing to do how we're getting along
Our minds are our own
Is that not where they belong?

Dreaming

You die a little bit every night as you age. And when you
   dream, you're in a combination of heaven and hell.

So live each waking day like you're in heaven, not hell.

Dreams can be hellaciously scary or heavenly blissful,
   and you have no control of them.

Think about that when you wake up from one of those
   dreams. "Which kind of day do you want to live today?"

I think when we are dreaming, it's as close to telepathy as we
   can get. So I hope you see me in your dreams, 'cause I've
   seen you in mine. Better yet, why don't you plan on it.

I don't know how to stop loving you the way I do. I don't know why or when you stopped loving me. And how is it that I love you now more than ever? I feel like I've gone from your best friend to an alien overnight. You're getting farther and farther away with each day. I wish I had a chance to see into your heart a little more.

Why didn't you come to me sooner? Don't you think I would have been scared of how serious you were, enough to want to do anything to make things right?

And would have and still will that's the saddest part. That's not fair play. You're supposed to talk to your man not hint around. We don't get that! We need visual, loud noises, hand waving, big signals and red + green lights. I never got any of those.

Given our time spent together don't you think our relationship deserved a serious working out together period? It doesn't happen on a one way street. I would do anything in the world for you. But you never shouted it out loud. If you keep things to yourself for too long you lose control. And that's what's happening here. Why did you keep this from me for so long?

The years you've been across the lake have been hard on both of us, I know that. Together surviving but, now I'm really blindsided with this! I know you're sorry but I still feel lied and cheated on. You turn off, walk away and want to be friends. If that's your wish, okay. I won't risk losing you as a friend. I've lost enough of you already.

Monday's Dishes

Monday's dishes are still in the sink
Now I know love really does stink
The weekend is here and I have one desire
Without your love I'm wallowing in the mire.
Since the day you left my world's turned cold
My heart feels like it's been bought and sold
I know from the cup of your love I cannot drink
Because I can't even find a glass in my sink
You told me you didn't feel that way for me anymore
Since then I haven't been able to get up off the floor
To look in your eyes and not see my flame.
I guess I only have myself to blame
Truly our love was really something great
Sometimes this knowledge comes too late
I'll try to live without you by my side
But this empty feeling will be hard to hide
When I get up from this floor and I'm out and about
You will always be on my mind there is no doubt.
Wherever I go, whatever I do
I know I always be thinking of you
I am the brightest star in the sky looking at you with a wink
But for now the dishes keep piling up in my sink
Can't wash my love for you off my skin
Wouldn't even know where to begin
As you move on and are busy with your new life
In my heart you will always be my wife
With that said you know how I think
The dishes of our last supper of love are forever in my sink!

Wearing Tears

When the pain becomes unbearable
The tears become wearable
When you left I became invisible
My love for you is irreplaceable
Your lack of love is inconceivable
The fact of your absence is unbelievable
How I react is uncontrollable
Look at my face it's so show-able
I thought our love was so delectable.
I didn't think I was so reject-able
Now you're gone I feel like a vegetable
What's left of my soul is negotiable
My world has become despair-able
I don't want to sound ascribable
Just can't believe this is irrevocable
My fuel for you is still flammable
Borderline committable
No secret here it's announce-able
My love for you is accountable
Your love for me is not as share-able
That's why these tears are my wearable

Year-round Yearning Blues

I'm not a seasonal man
That's never been my plan
So as long as you are gone
I'll just sit here on the lawn
I got the "year-round yearning blues"
Don't mind standing in the rain
Scorching sun and all its pain
I'll wait around night and day
Hoping you'll come my way
Still got the "year-round yearning blues"
Can't really tell how long it will take
Maybe I'm making a big mistake
But until I see your face
I'm staying in this space.
Here comes more "year-round yearning blues"
Critters creeping around at night
With thoughts of you I have no fright
So I'll stay here every day
For you is all I pray.
Can't shake the "year-round yearning blues"
Standing here up against a tree
Oh where, oh where, can my love be
September March or May
It could be any day
It's always, "year-round yearning blues"
Time goes by and I feel the same.
The wind reminds me of your name
The birds fly over me
You are the only thing I see
When I have the "year-round yearning blues."

Clean Sheets Without You

It's been 35 days since I last washed my sheets.
Losing you from that bed is one of my greatest defeats.
Our last time together I'll never forget.
Not seeing what you were missing I'll always regret
They say "nothing lasts forever but the earth and sky"
But the love I have for you is going to "make that a lie"
No matter where you are, with whom or what you do
There will always be a piece of me hanging out with you.
As I lie here alone in this dirty bed
I can't get the vision of you from my head
Your beauty goes far beyond my belief.
Not being next to it is absolute grief.
I can't begin to count the things that I miss
Guess you can call them all one big bliss.
That's a huge void I cannot replace
Especially if I can't ever kiss your face.
When I reach over in the dead of night.
Knowing you're not there fills me with fright
At some point I know I'll have to change my bed.
Clean sheets without you I will always dread.
Should hang them outside but I really don't care
"The memory of your smell is better than fresh air"

Funny thing about poem/song writing, every one is different in how it starts, how it ends, and how it's titled. Sometimes you start with a title, sometimes just a line, but they are all inspired by something or someone.

"Heart, pen and paper" started with just a line and wasn't titled until the end. I was going to call it Can't Escape Her. I still might. Same concept with "The Fall."

"Anytime I Cry" started with a title but "Year Round Yearning Blues" started with a title that was concocted by going through the dictionary and the word yearning was right on top of year-round and it went into a blues number. Some are inspired by obvious reasons, looking at my lack of housekeeping. I was talking through a fan which was pointed at my seedlings to add CO_2 to their diet.

Sometimes the title comes after the fact. Sometimes just changing one line, the whole meaning is changed to another occasion.

A Sobering Moment

Looking outside its starting to snow
I can tell which way the wind will blow.
I headed towards the door – it didn't feel right
Maybe it had to do with something last night.
As I opened the door, to my surprise
A six-foot bear staring straight in my eyes!
I didn't panic, but I had to think –
Wish I didn't have so much to drink.
He looked at me, I looked at him,
I just couldn't help myself starting to grin.
Just when I thought I was gonna be lunch,
I hurled in his face like a great big punch.
That's when I knew I had to move quick,
But then he stood close and began to lick.
I knew I wasn't dead 'cause I saw his breath,
Thought I might get sick, but there was nothing left.
He sniffed and he slurped; I saw his incisor –
Lucky for me that bear liked Budweiser!

Smoke Marijuana

We all went out to Denver to
   score some real good grass
Golden Nuggets straight from heaven
   were in our hands at last.
But driving home through the desert
   the car ran out of gas
The first thing we better do is
   try some of the stash.
And we'll smoke marijuana
   fire up the Dobie smoke marijuana

Luck would have it a town was nearby
   about a 6-mile walk
We tried to put our heads together
   and have a little talk
Looking over in the town's direction we
   all decided to balk.
Munchies hit us in about an hour and we knew we had to walk.
   but not before we smoke marijuana
Fire up that bowl
Smoke marijuana.

We finally made it to Seven Eleven
   potato chips galore.
Then bought enough to feed an army
   and headed out the door.
Walking back in Twinkie Heaven to the car at last.
Sitting around in a pile of crumbs I think we forgot the gas.
I guess it's time to smoke marijuana
Fire up that Bong
Smoke marijuana.

Just Put It Out There

You don't need a date to go see the Dead.

You don't need a knife to butter your bread.

Only need a beat to start moving your feet.

Just wait and see, you're in for a treat.

Have no care for a chair.

Best leave it over there.

Don't need no hair to put it out there.

The band is your date, so don't be late.

Happy ending, maybe sad

Either way it will always be great.

Sexual Tension on the Floor

Why is there always competition when you're on the floor to dance?
Can't it just be about the band and us instead of some romance?
We should all be having fun and being free.
Why does it have to be about he and she?
Sexual tension can distract you from the band.
It will pull you in like quicksand.
Just listen to the music and make your own move.
Forget about anybody else's groove
Let the band be in control of your feet
Into ourselves we must retreat.
So put on your blinders and get out of your chair
Put it down on the floor like you haven't a care.

Love Is It

Love is a prize. If you don't play for it, you can't win it.
I know how to lose it. I was just smack in it.
Some people tell you what you can do with it.
It's really hard but I think I want back in it.
Heartbreak will come, you just can't fight it.
The flame is still there, you need someone to light it.
You took your love away now I'm without it.
To the women of the world I just want to shout it.
Love is for real, nobody can deny it.
I'm telling you now, please don't doubt it.
There are people that think they can flout it.
Those are the ones that don't want to be in it.
We were created in love, in death I still want to be in it.
The Fab Four were right that's all you need is it.
                      it is all you need
                              it is all you need
                                        it is all you need

I like to have fun with my family on holidays and over the years have recited my poems specific to those. I do like to have fun sometimes.

Because we're all here in this fine way
It's time to eat Thanksgiving Day.
A turkey here a turkey there.
It's just enough for us to share.
Really don't have to understand.
It's what's been done across this land.
So if you're feeling blue this year.
Just kick it in another gear.
When seasons come and seasons go.
Our family love will always show.
So even though we're all not here.
Our collective thoughts are quite clear.
And when we're done we'll all be full.
Of love and food so keep your cool
So when the day comes to an end
Love to you we all want to send.
In our hearts we might want to pray
That every day is Thanksgiving Day!

Turkey Day is here at last
I hope we don't get too much gas.
Some beans, some squash, oh where do I start?
Sorry I forgot that those make us fart.
As we look across the table in stares
We ate too much to get out of our chairs.
Pumpkin pie and ice cream like Romeo & Juliet
Hope the line tomorrow is not too long for the toilet.
But enough about functional food that's not why we're here.
It's for being with the people that we hold dear.
For those who can't be here and we can't be there.
Let's just send a little something through the air.

The Easter Bunny has a Problem this Year

Here comes Peter Cotton Tail
Drinking down a pint of ale.
Sip-ity- Sip-ity- off the trail he goes.
Got no chocolate not one single treat
Can't even stand up on his feet
Trip-ity – trip-ity over the bank he goes.
There goes Peter Cotton Tail
Heading down town for some cold Pale Ale
Zig-idy zag-idy
That's just the way he goes.
Colored eggs filled with cash
Lost them all when he fell on his ass
Slip-ity – slip-ity in the street he goes.

Here comes Peter Cotton Tail
Drinking down a pint of ale
Sip-ity sip-ity
Guess we'll see how next year goes.

Most poetry is inspired by something stronger than ourselves. Might be the feeling you get from your favorite music or maybe the feeling you get from a loss of love or life. I would like to dedicate this collection of my open soul to my late grandma Franny of 101 years

I wrote this for grandma Franny's 100th birthday party.

P. S. Any of you musicians out there looking for words here I am.

Hope you enjoyed my genuine pain and suffering through the rhyme.

To the first centurion in our life
Your love is as sharp as a fine chef's knife.
As we gather here for your special day.
You've showed us each something in your own way.
Generations give us our separate lives.
But to be like you we will attempt to strive.
You are in our hearts every day and night.
That feeling is something you just can't fight.
Sometimes the weight of the world we all share.
Wisdom from you makes us lighter than air.
When life gets us down and we just don't know.
Thinking of you gives us get up and go.
Life is a journey on a great big bus.
Thanks for the fare you have given us.
God put you here to stand the tests of time.
To walk in your shoes must be quite sublime.
Memories of you can make us all strong.
For one hundred years is not very long.
You told us that life can be very grand.
This is the plane that we don't want to land.
Before it is time for us to leave town.
Your love's in us all so just look around.
Now there is only one more thing to say.
And that's HIP-HIP_HORAY it's Franny's Day.

I don't recommend divorce for anyone unless it's mutual. Even then the scars stay deep. The lives of two can affect many. Sorry, but I must sign off with the bad note it was intended to be Divorced Poetically.

Enjoy…

Deadly Broken Heart

There are so many things in life that can kill you.
But "nothing is more deadly than a broken heart."
You can make a plan that might defend you.
When it comes to love if you're in it it's from the start.
As I walk with my heart broken in two.
My blood will spill as I think of you
While I bleed on this floor today
Only half of me is alive to say.
"Nothing is more deadly than a broken heart"
Absolutely nothing on this planet

Since I've lost the best.
There is no rest.
You're my four leaf clover.
Now our love is over.
Don't know how this can be real
It's a scab I just can't peel.
Love in or Love out—it's all a la carte
Nothing is more deadly than a broken heart.

So if you're not sure which way you should go.
Take the right chance and let it flow.
When you've been stung before and you're getting it again.
You know love's pain really has no end.
Might try and hide but you can't out-smart
Nothing is more deadly than a broken heart.
Not a damned thing.

The risks of love are high as a mountain
When obtained it's like a magic fountain
And if you lose love's highest peak
You get your lowest at best bleak.
It's up to you to decide
You can slip or you can slide
Either way you're going to fall
It's not our choice after all
Someday it will hit you like a dart.
Nothing is more deadly than a broken heart.
Absolutely nothing in this world.

What's more deadly than a broken heart?
Absolutely nothing say it again
What's more deadly than a broken heart?
Absolutely nothing.

Keep My Soul

My soul left with you now I'm here without a prayer.
To get it back from some other I really don't care.
It's you I signed up for to walk through Love's Door.
If you end up with someone else those thoughts I can't
    explore.
As the days go by and the nights become longer than ever.
To let you go all the way is too hard of an endeavor.

So you can keep my soul it has no place here.
You can keep my soul gonna make it quite clear.
You can keep my soul you're my only true dear.
You can keep my soul with you year after year.

When I said I'd love you forever I wasn't telling a lie
I just was expecting to be right next to you until I die
Don't know what a soul looks like but I know it's not here
It's hanging out with you just a whisper in your ear.
Life gives you choices some you make on your own.
Gave you the ones I had these exhibits I have shown.

So please keep my soul it has no place here.
You can keep my soul gonna make it quite clear.
You can keep my soul you're my only true dear.
You can keep my soul with you year after year.

They say time can heal every kind of pain
What's missing inside I don't want to explain
The further away you are the better it is for me
To watch you hold another I can't bear to see
Gave it up to you so long ago
Without you there's nothing to show
Might as well flush it down the drain.

But I'd rather you keep my soul it has no place here
You can keep my soul gonna make it quite clear.
You can keep my soul you're my only true dear.
You can keep my soul with you year after year.

Now you're far away and I'm by myself.
It's going with you or sitting on a shelf
I can't express my feelings for you to anyone out loud
If I speak then the tears fall as if I were a cloud.
On this paper I share all my soul has to know.
It doesn't want to shine ever since you had to go.

So go ahead and keep my soul it has no place here.
You can keep my soul gonna make it quite clear.
You can keep my soul you're my only true dear.
You can keep my soul with you year after year.

What's in a Name

The mere mention of your name
Makes me just about insane.
You've taken my love out of your game.
That's why these tears fall like rain.
There's no way of getting you off my brain.
Know you didn't intend to cause me so much pain.
This is too much for my soul. I really can't explain.
My heart is so heavy, you need to pick it up with a crane.
I feel my life is slipping down a spiral drain.
Not only hit, I'm being dragged by this freight train
If it ever lets me go, I'll be walking with a cane.
Nothing can take me away, not even a jet airplane.
All the rain, pain, cranes, drains, planes, and trains
Wouldn't stop me from saying your name.
To lose your love is my ultimate shame.
Now I have only myself to blame.
It's impossible to extinguish this flame.
So I have to keep calling out your name.
My arrows of love will always fly with you in aim.
You see, there's really an awful lot in a name.

If I can just make it until tomorrow, then I can do the "second favorite thing" in the world. And that's attending live Rock & Roll music (up close and personal). But tonight I'm not doing a very good job of making sure I make it there. That's because I know my "first favorite thing" is not going to happen again. And that's to be there with you.

So now I have to move everything in my life back at least one step because you are still number one.

I hope I don't miss the show but my heart won't be in it all the way. And that's because I don't own all of my heart I lost most of it to you. Think I have "just enough to make it until tomorrow".

P. S. Thank God I made it to tomorrow!

Just Enough To Make It Until Tomorrow

My heart has "just enough to make it until tomorrow."
Even though it's going to be another day of sorrow.
Because you're not around
Can't get up off the ground
To turn back time I'd beg, steal or borrow.
Now I feel the pain inside my chest.
Just knowing that I lost the best.
I can't get you off my mind
Someone like you I'll never find.
What's left of my heart has only one quest.
Want to pump every drop of my blood,
    right on the floor under you.
But then I wouldn't have enough to do
    the things we do.
Because you've gone away
The pain is here to stay
Tomorrow don't know if my heart will have a clue
My heart gets weaker and weaker every day
As you get further and further away
Can feel it beating low
Why did you have to go?
I hope it has enough for another day.

Not One Chore

What should I wear
I really don't care
Piles of clothes everywhere
Can't find the floor
Where is the door
Since you've been gone
        haven't done one chore

Crumbs and Clothes

"Crumbs and clothes" all over the floor.
Been piling up since you walked out my door.
Don't seem to really care anymore.
Just getting through the day is a chore
My heart wasn't enough and you needed more.
So you took your love to another shore.
Now I'm left without the one I adore.
It hurts deep down into my core.
I don't even know what this broom is for.

Nothing Here For Me To See

I know I'll never get over you.
Doesn't matter what I have to do.
Until I can see your face,
I'm running in a losing race.
Makes no difference what I say,
I know your gonna stay away.
It's like not one single word
   that I've said have you heard.
You know I'm going to fall down
   just because you're not around.
When you're really low,
   solo is not the way to go.
If you're all together
   you can handle any weather.
Been nothing but sleet, rain, snow
   ever since you had to go.
Now I have to face reality.
Without your love my life's a 'calamity.
Life says the best is yet to come.
My best has left and with me she's done.
As I'm walking up the street,
I'll be looking down at my feet.
Because you're not in front of me.
There's *"nothing there for me to see"*.

Nothing's As Fun

Nothing's As Fun Without You
Don't know what I'm going to do.
Nothing's as fun without you.
My heart is now black and blue.
I feel the pain down to my shoe.
There's a sting in my eyes like I'm wearing shampoo.
If I try and do something that's new,
It's not going to be as fun without you.
Like shooting billiards without a cue.
Simmering inside me like a stew.
Feels like I'm captured in a zoo.
With you things were as sweet as honeydew.
But now nothing's as fun without you.

Truly Out of my Sight

The day you left me it was sunny and bright.
From that moment on, it's been dark as night.
You know I love you with all my might.
That's why I'll never give up the fight.
When I'm with you, I'm as high as a kite.
Now that you're gone, I can't hold back the dyke.
"Knowing you are truly out of my sight."
I don't seem to care about finding the light.
In my dreams, I can still hold you tight.
But without you here, my world has no height.
You can choke on love if you take too big a bite.
Nothing in life can give me more fright,
Than "knowing you are truly out of my sight."

Tears That I've Shed for You

If you could save every tear that I've shed for you.
It would fill all the world's oceans so deep and blue.
Because you are gone, my life has no glue.
The plan that I had was sticking with you.
Now you've decided to do something new.
What's on your mind, I just don't have a clue.
For you there is no end to what I will do.
Can't fight this feeling, I don't know Kung Fu.
There is no medicine for this kind of flu.
You are the one that turned us into two.
All I have left is memories and woo.
I'm sailing on life's ship without my best crew.
Riding the waves of "tears that I've shed for you."

Happy Almost Anniversary

It's been 102 days since you dropped the bomb on me. And it's been 59 days since I last saw you. I don't know if that was the last, and I pray it's not.

I spent five thousand three hundred + seventy three days in the wonder of love with you.

I got that one extra day with you to hold on to.

I don't know if I have another five thousand three hundred and seventy three days left. But if I do and or did I would trade them all for that single yesterday.

Now I will continue to count the days apart from you.

And I will *never* stop loving you.

Love's Reaction

Ever since your love was extracted
   only darkness I have attracted
When the sun is shining bright,
   that's all I see is the black of night.
Even though you're out of my sight,
   I'll never give up my fight.
This is how my love has reacted
   in my heart you're never subtracted

A Day Without Tears

"A day without tears" is rare
                           for me
My eyes are so wet I can
                           hardly see
Now that your gone for good, I
                           must survive.
I'm really not living, but I am alive.
When you left, so did the honey from
                           my hive.
Just as you're riding high, you take
                           a dive
My foolish heart thought it was our
                           time to arrive

HB

Because I've Bared My Soul

The pain that it took to bare my soul,
   has left me with a heart as black as coal.
The road you chose made me pay a heavy toll.
Now these tears fall for you with no control.
Since you've left my world has a great big hole.
As you drove away from me, my heart you stole.
Without your love my shoes have no sole.
Don't know if I can make it over the next knoll
Even with a full cup, I have an empty bowl.
Through life without you now I must stroll.
If luck could get you back, those dice I would roll.
My love flag flies for you upon the highest pole.
To be with you again, I'd give all I have to dole.
You know to love you only has always been my goal.
This is the pain I face "because I've bared my soul"

Splattering Tears

I never felt the rain in my brain.
Yet the flood from my eyes was more than the skies.
Now I'm barely afloat without a boat.
Only takes a minute to be swimming in it.
It's about to drive me insane.
If I close my eyes it doesn't matter.
There will always be these tears to splatter.
That's all I can say cause it happens every day
I have no life jacket, hope I don't see Nurse Ratchet.
But I think I need something for this pain.
Don't know when it's coming, but you do when it's there.
No way to stop it, couldn't try on a dare.
My watering eyes I can't disguise, what would it even matter.
Makes no difference where or when, these tears will always splatter.
There is no mop that could clean up this slop.
Don't think there's even a drain.
Any time day or night, it comes without a warning
All I do is long for you. It's like I'm always mourning
I'm trying hard to bake this cake, but something is wrong with the batter
The recipe is incomplete, now I'm in defeat
In my kitchen of life the tears do splatter!

            Day 99½

            HAB

The Fragility of My Soul

The fragility of my soul is that of an eggshell.
Now that you're gone I've been in heaven, now I'm in hell.
In my sea of tears, I am caught in a swell.
It won't let me go, this I can tell.
Together, I thought we had a good gel.
The pain inside me makes me want to yell!
It's written on my face, do I have to ring a bell?
As I'm thinking of you, staring down the wishing well.
To be with you again, what's left of my soul I would surely sell.
Since the day we met I can't seem to get up, because for you I fell.

Just a Little Shove

We all need to be in love
Some have to get a little shove
Not just anyone will do
Bright lights pale in front of you
Spent so many years in your arms
How could anyone match those charms?
Now I'm here in some strange place
And all I can see is your face
Looking around in this big room
There isn't one flower with your bloom
How much pain can one man take?
Not much left of my heart to break
Now I have to go and live my life
Knowing you don't want to be my wife.

The Empty Side of the Bed

Every day I have to drag myself out of bed.
I just can't get the vision of you from my head.
Without you here I'd rather go back to the dream instead.
As my feet hit the floor they're as heavy as lead.
My body is drained and it must be fed.
Through the night this broken heart has surely bled.
My pillow is wet from the tears that I shed.
Looking at the clock it's half past dead.
Lying here I can't make any bread.
Like a book I wish that I never read.
Things we wish were never said.
Places you hoped to never tread.
It's bad enough knowing we'll never be wed.
But to not get to see you is a world of dread.
I don't know how to get your vision from my head,
Or put someone else's vision there instead.
I should leave my feet up, I don't need the lead.
Can't find a way to get fed.
Not much left to be bled.
Still a few tears to be shed.
But the clock is no way dead.
Time for some butter on my bread.
Different things to be said.
A better story to be read, and places to tread.
The only way this world I won't dread
Is filling the empty side of my bed.

To Capture Your Gaze

When my love light left, to the curb my heart was tossed
The world's king's ransoms couldn't cover the cost.
Now I know what it's like to be lost.
Just thinking it without drinking it, gets me sauced
Out of your sight, you made sure I was flossed.
Yet I will never regret the day our paths crossed.

Now that you're gone I must mend my ways.
Surely ahead there must be better days.
But euphoria with you is strong as purple haze.
Now only my memory can capture your gaze.
I pray each day that you'll get over this phase
Don't know if I'll ever get out of this maze
Talking like this might be the latest craze.
In the pasture of your love is where I want to graze.
What we had together, for me will always amaze

The Day You Got Going

This heart has been stolen without my knowing.
My soul is beat and swollen since the day you got going.
Now my days are spent all alone.
Without you near, it's not the same by phone.
If words could make you change your mind.
You are all I ever needed to find.
My flood of tears has kept on flowing,
    ever since the day you got going.
There is no warning for this kind of pain.
It comes so fast, like a speeding train.
On a scale of one to ten, I hurt *eleven*!
If I'm not holding your hand, what use is heaven?
To the world, my love for you I've been showing,
    even after the day you got going.
I've had bright days and dark ones too.
But they all seem better standing beside you.
There must be a cloud hanging over me.
Raining tears from my eyes, getting hard to see.
Gale winds of woe haven't stopped blowing,
    ever since "the day you got going"

Just Me And Not You

How can I explain this pain in my heart?
It just won't stop, since you had to part.
I guess it's like a knife in the chest.
Just knowing that I've lost the best
It's been so long since I've seen your face.
Minus your love, I feel left out of the race.
If I ever get to see you again
I'll make sure not to let go of your hand
What went wrong, and when did it go?
How could I tell? You never let it show.
I know this feeling is not going to end.
I'm not even going to try and pretend.
Right now my life's biggest fear,
Is knowing I can't hold you near.
Without you here nothing seems right,
Even the sun doesn't shine bright.
What can I say, you are my everything.
I'm still waiting for you to wear my ring.
People think I'm crazy, but I don't care.
You're the one I want for my life to share.
When my nightmare ends I may wake up in hell.
Sleeping without you is worse, this I will tell.
This is the hardest thing I ever had to do.
Walking through this world with just me and not you.

Lost What I Lack

All the roads I could have chosen instead.
It was yours, and down I went as you led.
Now it's time to find my way back,
To the point where I lost what I lack.
But my soul is locked in an abandoned shack.
What's beating in my chest is under attack.
Nobody knows just how much I have bled,
Because you've decided that we shouldn't wed.
The world looks so different without you around.
In any direction, there's no one like you to be found.
Somehow I followed you way off track.
Can't seem to find where I lost what I lack.
As I try to walk without your hand in mine.
Everything is foreign, I can't read the sign.
I push myself forward into each day,
Looking for someone to show me the way.
Without the light of your eyes, I can't see
Just exactly where I'm supposed to be.
Down the hill, lost my Jill, leaving without "Jack."
Going out of my mind, trying to find,
Where I "lost what I lack."

Just My Hurl

I'm so low down over losing my girl.
If I start to think of her I just might hurl.
Now my life is in a mess.
And I'm ready to confess
Don't know if I can give love another whirl.
I can't seem to get it together,
Knowing you won't be with me forever.
Now I'm sitting here alone
Waiting by the phone.
When will I stop loving you? The answer is *Never!*

Glad To Sad

I went from really glad to suicidal sad overnight
What we had wasn't bad, there was no need for flight.
The time it takes to change a life,
Comes in a wink of an eye.
The worse my time has come I know,
Ever since you said goodbye
Looking out in this world all alone,
You're nowhere in sight.
To never see you again, I have no greater fright
I know it's time to say goodbye,
But I really just can't do it.
I wish I had another change. The last one I guess I blew it.

Ragged Over You

Every day I hurt more and more
Because you're not here for me to adore.
Some days I don't want to go out the door
This is a space I don't want to explore.
I'm cut wide open to the core.
My heart is laid out on the floor.
Without your love my soul cannot soar.
I don't know if I can live without you to love.
Just standing on some ledge waiting for that shove.
Now you're gone, I'm going to fall like a wing clipped dove.
I'm losing my faith in the one up above.
Whatever, wherever, whoever, it's you I'll be thinking of.
My subjection to rejection is a reflection of my obsession
    with you.
Your disappearance has caused an interference with my
    appearance because now I'm ragged over you.
I'm trying to stop writing about you,
But I can't seem to do it.
When it comes to your love, I wasn't quite through with it

I cry every day over you. It's been 239 days in a row. Every morning I tell myself, I'm not going to cry today. But something, someone or someplace reminds me of you or us. Then I just *burst* into tears.

The reminders of you are endless and constant. Every flower on the planet for starters!

Example: I've been using the same can of shaving cream you gave me, for over 250 days. Seemed almost magical. It just ran out, and I *burst*, I got some cookbooks for soup. But when I started to read through them, I thought you would like these. I'm not going to make soup. Who am I kidding? I got them for you. *Burst again*. Walking through the grocery store for no reason. Looking for something to cook, and I stop at all your favorites. *Burst* right in the store. If I see people walking hand in hand, just about anywhere. *I'm done.* Even if I'm driving sometimes I have to pull over to *shake it off.*

And songs: I can't even count how many that I can't listen to without crying. Even at live shows it's hard to hold back. Another reason I like front row at concerts is nobody but the band sees me cry.

I was putting on Chapstick and thought of your lips. Burst into tears and right out of it into a poem

Lips, Hips and Your Brain

Without your hips, lips, and brain
My life's work is all down the drain.
For all I really ever wanted to be,
Is the man with you standing next to me.
Why is your body not up against mine?
Because you're gone there's no fruit on my vine.
There's nobody else that's on my mind.
It's only you, there is no other kind.
Deserts, canyons, and the mighty seas
I need your love to cross them with ease.
Feel like I'm falling then drowning in abyss.
It's your "*lips, hips and brain*" I truly miss.
To hold you in my arms again.
In my dreams I can pretend
So many things remind me of you.
They're stuck to me with crazy glue
What continues to cause me to go insane
Is not being around your "*lips, hips and brain*"

If I ordered a small hot and sour soup and asked for it in a large bowl. I think I might fill it up with tears before I ate it all. I have dripped tears into my bowls before. As a matter of fact I've showered many of plates of food. If I eat by myself, which is often, tears are my *seasoning*. Oh I feel a song coming out of one word.

Seasoning My Dinner With Tears

I'm seasoning my dinner with tears.
I'm thinking of all our years.
I'm walking around with fears.
People look at me with leers.
I don't see us in any mirrors.
It's not even me that appears
There's a constant pain that just sears.
It's still there after a hundred beers.
With the beating of my heart it interferes
This is surely one of the worst frontiers
I'm getting no help from my peers
Once I start crying the plate disappears
That's why I'm "*seasoning my dinner with tears*"

"True story but don't try this at home "too salty" "not good for blood pressure" "not good anything"

Can't Be Me Without We

No one will ever hold my heart but you.
If you got a good man best stick to him like glue.
You wouldn't want him to end up like me.
Drowning in tears deep as the sea.
Pain that never lets you be.
Like a cat stuck up in a tree.
A dog that won't stop scratching a flea.
I just can't be me if there is no we.
Without your love I have no purpose.
I'm just a sad clown working the circus.
You left my mountains to put your feet in the sand.
There isn't a lovelight like you in this whole land.
Your eyes are my world, now I can't see
You locked up my heart, I don't have a spare key
To have and hold then lose, is an expensive fee.
For all my life it's you I want to tag along.
Now I'm like a bird without a song
Trapped in a cage never free
That's why I can't be me without we.

What Else Can I Strive?

These empty arms miss your charms.
This broken heart wasn't very smart.
Why did I ever let you leave?
Waking up without you, I just can't believe.
I wish you'd come back,
Before I have a heart attack
This pain will never go away,
Until you're back to stay.
What's going on inside me is hard to explain.
But I do know exactly what's causing the pain.
Bad as standing in the freezing rain,
While being hit by a train.
Losing you while it was cold,
Makes it hard to want to grow old.
A roof over my head, things shouldn't seem hopeless.
But living without you, I feel like I'm homeless.
I'm working so hard just to survive.
If not for your love, what else can I strive?

Life As I Knew It

I've never felt this much pain in my life.
Wouldn't feel a thing if I was cut by a knife.
I'm going to bleed out on the floor.
Because you walked right out of my door,
And won't make love with me anymore.
The needs I have must now be with a stranger
You've shown me love holds way too much danger
Now I'm going down a one way,
Just because you're not here today.
Don't know if I'll ever see you again.
Life as I knew it, has already come to an end.
I guess the burden lays on me.
Must have been too blind to see.
You always had your very own plan.
And I wasn't gonna be your #1 man.
If not for you it is for me.
You are the only one I want to see.
Time is supposed to heal, no sign of it yet.
When it comes to love there is no forgive and forget.
So stay as far away from me as you can.
Especially if you're with another man.
I'm not the same person since you went away.
Don't even know how far I've gone astray.
Because you're not here it's really not clear,
   how I'll make it through this year.
I don't want someone else's love to defend.
Life as I knew it, has already come to an end.

Shitty Fan

I want your new man to break your heart.
Wish it for you right from the start.
I'd give him all I made in my entire life,
    not to ask you to be his wife.
Because when he leaves you'll feel like me.
Maybe then you'll really see,
    what true love is supposed to be.
My thoughts for you flow like *no tomorrow*.
The reality of that brings only sorrow.
Just knowing you're with another man.
Can't get out of the way of this "shitty fan."

P. S. It's set at high speed/volume flowing right at me.

What's Left to Behold?

There's nothing left for me to behold.
Because you're gone before we grew old.
Now my soul has been bought and sold.
I'm standing out in the freezing cold.
It's so cold as I cry out loud.
Tears cover me like a frozen shroud.
The wind keeps blowing in waves of fear.
It may keep going year after year.
On a scale of 1-10, I now hurt 110.
Because you went away, this pain is here to stay.
As I lay in my bed full of dread.
Can't get our last talk out of my head.
Your lack of words, the truth they did tell.
What they meant, put me straight in hell.
While making you they broke the mold.
Now there is nothing left for me to behold.

Tie-Dye

I've been wearing, at some point
   in my day a tie-dye T-shirt every
   day (not the same one) since the
   love of my life left me in
   the "cold rain and snow."
Today was 255 days since she
   had to go.
Now I only have a dozen shirts.
It's kind of my flag to show how much it hurts.

HB

My Messed Up Dead Head Dream

We were in Philly city after a Dead show. I don't know why there but I felt it. We were in my Buick. I stopped the car for directions. While talking to a woman (that turned out to be a hooker) she gave me an unexpected kiss. You saw that and went running and screaming at me into the city. I tried to talk to you but you kept going on and onward.

A gang of men with a huge black guy that looked like Mike Tyson (no I wasn't ruffed) (I told him he looked like Mike at some point in the confrontation); stepped in. You stayed with him and his men wouldn't let me near you. As you held onto Bubba (no joke I think that was his name) they took us to a huge building with steps outside. As Bubba's men kept me outside, the two of you went upstairs. I broke away from the gang and chased you and Bubba. I got inside and another gang grabbed me and took me to a room, and sat me in front of a large window overlooking the river. I was yelling and crying out your name, but you and Bubba were out of sight. They made me sit on a Priest's lap (so weird) to tell the truth. I was crying and telling our story. They all started to cry. (No, this is not a comedy. It's a nightmare).

Then the Priest said let him go. Then the building started to move into the water. We were on a giant cruise ship that looked like a courthouse from the outside. They told me I was too late because Bubba had left the boat already. I was screaming and crying and I wanted to jump through the window to the water. They told me the water was too cold and I would freeze to death. Everyone was crying (including the Priest, how weird).

Somehow I forced my way out to wake up with tears in my eyes and sweating. No way was I going back to sleep that dawn.

Somehow at the very "point of no return" my body knew it was a dream. In that dream, I was so upset that I woke myself up.

I'm so scared to know who you may be with at this point, it might as well be Big Bubba.

In the dream I was armed with only a tire iron against 4 or 5 guys and Big Bubba. (Terrifying) I'm afraid to go to sleep alone tonight.

> The relief of waking up is brief.
> The reality of what it means is grief.

My publisher has been asking me to resubmit my work before the holidays. I told them I didn't know how they would go for me. I might be emotionally inspired to write more. It didn't take long for sad to come back even harder. So I'm sending you a few of my latest unedited, untyped pieces of work.

By the way, that's what I feel like these days. I have it all in one place except for the cover. I have my final page, but I keep putting more work in front. I do want this to end soon. I truly hope you never feel this kind of pain.

Better Than Nothin'

As much as my words might say.
My love for you "WILL NOT FADE AWAY"
So if you can find it in your heart
   from my life, don't make a complete depart.
Doesn't have to be often, could be any sunny day.
The light from your baby blues,
   will brighten up my day.
Being left so far behind, is the hardest place.
Especially if I never get to see your face.
So call me anytime night or day.
For you I'll always have something to say.

To talk to you from afar, is "better than nothin',"
   now that someone else is taking care of your muffin.
Had to throw that in there, I hope it made you smile.
Time to look for my heart, at the bottom of the circular file.
Just because you're not going to be my wife.
Doesn't mean you have to disappear from my life.

H

Don't Want No Christmas Tree

Another Christmas Day bringing lots of joy.
A smiling face on every girl and boy.
Family and friends gather with cheer.
Now that you're gone, I won't feel it this year.
Just want to disappear or go and hide.
Don't know when these tears will subside.
Holidays don't mean as much to me anymore.
That's because I'm not with the one I adore.
It's a feeling you just can't replace.
Deep in my chest there is an empty space.
There will be no Christmas tree for me.
As long as you're not here for me to see.
Something will always be wrong with this day.
Still don't know why you had to go away.
You left me standing here all alone.
I feel the chill right to my bone.
The warmth of your arms are gone forever.
To get through this day will be an endeavor.
So Merry Christmas to head honcho elf.
I feel like spending this one by myself.

Christmas

I'm going to spend the money I would have spent on you and your family, on the homeless. That's the way I feel without you. "Homeless"

Lost My Number One

Yet another trip around the sun.
This one wasn't very much fun.
You see, I've lost my number one.
For me, this world has come undone.
From this pain, I cannot run.
All my love, you chose to shun.
There is someone else that you call hun.
You still have some, and I have none.
Feels like I'm dragging around a ton.
This isn't funny, it's a very bad pun.
I'm at the OK corral without a gun.
In the game of love, I have not won.
Because I lost my number one.

There Still Can Be Bliss

As I lay awake alone in my bed,
Just knowing you're not alone torments my head.
I can't seem to find any peace in my soul.
Since you left, I've been trapped in a hole.
Your cup flows over, I have an empty bowl.
You're still shining bright, I'm black as coal.
You have another.
I'm still under cover.
It's really not fair.
For you I still care.
I hope our history repeats itself.
Until then my heart remains on the shelf.
So look around as much as you need.
I'll always be here when you don't succeed.
No matter who comes into your life,
I still want you for my wife.
It's crazy isn't it, after all this?
That I think there still can be bliss.

I believe dealing with divorce is harder than a death. You have to accept death because she's gone forever. But divorce the acceptance factors are unbalanced. One side is always worse off. I'm on the down side of the scale. I can't accept the fact that the love of my life is with another man. It's sheer torture. You can't do anything about death. With divorce you may not in reality be able to do anything, but you think you can and you want to try. The percentages are not in your favor by far, yet desperation sets in. Love is the most powerful drug on the planet. It's built right into every one of us. We are all desperate to be in love forever. Those that are lucky enough, are still desperate not to lose that. But when forever is cut short, it's hard to handle being without that drug. Unfortunate for me the torture continues, because I still love who I lost.

HB

No Need to Wrap It

I was not really excited about or at any of my weddings.
But I would about and at ours.
Now I'm not excited about or at the time spent without
   you, turning minutes into hours.
I'm not that excited about spring coming and all its flowers.
Because you're gone I'm not excited about or at the fact
   of losing all my powers.
I'm not excited about not being able to climb your towers,
   or not being able to share your showers.
But I am excited about "anything that's still ours".
I'll take it! No need to wrap it.
Whatever you got for me, I'll take it.

 You Always

HB

That Thing

You're the inspiration to everything I do
I would never have learned to live, if it wasn't for you.
Without you close by, don't know how I'll get through.
On the sunniest of days my sky is not blue.
There's a feeling inside me like I drank a strange brew.
What have I gone and done?
Now I'm back to square one.
Without you life is not as fun.
So it seems again, I have not won.
You took my heart and you're back on the run.
Freedom you have, yet still I have none.
Dragging this anchor, my ship sails towards the sun.
I'll always hold onto this thing that we've done.

P. S. When can we do it again and again and again?

If It Wasn't For You

I won't let you get all the way out of my life.
Even though I still want you to be my wife.
Dundee himself couldn't cut me with a bigger knife.
There's nothing left of my resolve,
   since you made our love dissolve.
Both my heart and soul you did involve.
My thoughts for you flow through the day.
This love for you I won't throw away.
No matter how much it makes me pay.
If your heart has any space left for me,
   tell me now or let it be.
For my locked up heart, there is one key.
As I open my eyes you're all I want to see.
The impossible dream, it's out there, maybe true.
Wouldn't even exist "if it wasn't for you."

My Inside Hurts Way More Than My Out

Sometimes it makes me want to shout!
I still find it hard to say her name.
And that just might be a crying shame.
I'll love her forever there is no doubt.
That's really what it's all about.
She can make her own rules for her own game
But for me she's still my only dame.
Now I'm in a world where she's no longer my cloute.
That's why my inside hurts way more than my out.

I thought what we had was an amazing thing
Just being in love is like a bell you can ring.
Now that she's gone I can't hear a sound
Nothing to ring about cause she's not around.
Knowing I would lose I'd still take the same route.
That makes my inside hurt way more than my out.

Speaking of bells love is like the pepper I'll tell ya fellow
Sometimes green sometimes red, now I'm stuck in the yellow
My tears continue like an endless spout
And I'm hurting inside way more than out.

Just About to Choke

Be aware of who you love, don't be someone's joke
When you think you got it right, you're just about to choke.
These words I've written are just for you.
Through this phone my cracked voice comes through.
I really have nothing else to do.
I'll die pretending we're really not through.

There is nothing like black and white.
Put it down on a page, get it right.
Some things are really hard to say.
Put them on paper, it will be okay.

I just can't write about this much more.
If I don't stop soon I won't get off the floor.
Time to move along.
Too much of the same song.
I'm sure there will be more to say.
It's just always going to be that way.
The jagged lightning bolt through my heart.
Left a scar forever since the day you did part.

For You I Bide

Since you left, it's been really hard to hide.
It's plain for everyone to see, I'm dying inside.
You stripped me of my heart, soul and pride.
Been searching so far and wide.
Can't find anyone to confide.
Nobody wants to hear my side.
My tongue is twisted and tied.
So I write to get it off my hide.
Without you here, I have no guide.
I told you forever, I never lied.
But you I guess, could not abide.
My brain is boiling, scrambled then fried.
This story has only one side.
Oh yes, very hard I have cried.
Enough tears to raise up the tide.
No matter how long, for you I bide.
For your love, I'll continue my vied.
I'll always want you for my bride.

Walking Hand in Hand

As I try to find just the right word.
There is important information to be heard.
So if you're listening with your heart.
When you love someone, find a way not to part.
To all the people across this land.
Make sure you're *"walking hand in hand."*
The world needs more of this kind of transportation!

HB

Uphill, Downhill

To make it to the next day takes all I have
My wounds are always open with no bandage or salve.
Without the love of my life, its been an uphill strife.
With every uphill step I take, it's a downhill direction I make.
My love for you is never fake.
Even if you think we were a mistake.
I still want to see you when I wake.
The ashes are still hot, you'll need an iron rake
Because your gone, my body does ache.
The tears from my eyes could fill a Great Lake.
Frozen from the sky, you are my only snowflake
Without you there my birthdays will have no cake.
This is the worst I've felt, for Christ sake.
I'm swallowed up in loves earthquake.
There's nothing left of my heart to break
With every uphill step I take,
It's a downhill direction I make.

Not Wearing My Ring

The woman I love has given me the shove.
In two she split my heart, ever since her depart.
My feet feel like they're concrete.
I can barely get across the street.
Dragging myself all over town.
I feel the tears, for I am that clown.
Sometimes it hits me without a warning.
Like a tidal size wave of morning
Not sure if I'll ever swim free
Still looking for your hand to grab hold of me.
Just knowing we're not living together anymore
In any direction I can't see the shore.
When the wave subsides, I'll be back on land.
It will never be the same if I'm not holding your hand.
Now it seems I've lost my soul.
Losing you I pay a heavy toll.
The world around me is dark and grey
For loving you too much, this price I pay.
Don't think I ever hear the birds sing.
Because I know your not wearing my ring.

Even If My Eyes Could No Longer See

Even if my eyes could no longer see,
It would be your voice I'd want speaking to me.
Nothing in this world is like your smell,
These are only some of the reasons I fell.
In the presence of your aura I want to dwell.
Without you around it's a living hell.
A thousand coins for you tossed in the wishing well.
There's nothing here but the truth to tell.
You're still the only girl for me.
Even if my eyes could no longer see.

My Sales Pitch of Wisdom

Suck it up gentlemen and ladies.

No matter what they might say ("it matters") the more money you have to spend on your loved one for V-day the more you should.

In reality "it's only money not honey". Aren't they worth every penny and dollar? Even if you have to take some away from every other holiday to save for V-day.

It's better than D-day.

> It's time to be they, time to say yeh.
> Time to roll in the hay, it's time for V-day.
> V-day is a bright day, D-day is a dark day.
> V-day is a hooray day, D-day is don't say day.
> V-day is here to stay day, D-day is get on your way day.
> By investing in V-day you can avoid losing it all on D-day.
> Spend the time and money on the honey,
> V-day — it's way better than D-day.

Not Just Something I Ate

I love her so much now I'm the one I hate.
That's because I found this out too late.
The person you love is not someone you rate.
It's the one who really opens the gate.
Sometimes there's a gap in how to communicate
Love in itself does not involve fate.
Some of us only can sit and wait.
So now I'm here like a dog in a crate.
Wishing she would just corroborate.
Then we can get back and copulate.
I know our time together was always great.
My passion for her I could never obliterate.
She's part of me, not just something I ate.
With her I always tried to correlate.
This is a feeling I cannot exaggerate.
Her leaving me I did not instigate.
To hold her again I would not hesitate
My love for her is always deliberate.
I tried to make it quite instantiate.
I thought we were a perfect aggregate.
With her is all I want to obligate.
Nothing in my life feels more legitimate.
My feelings for her remain obdurate
I don't know why she cannot coordinate
Without love this world you cannot mitigate.
There is no way your going to moderate.
You must always find the right commensurate.
Living without her I never did contemplate.
Now in my life there is no consummate.
For myself I do commiserate.
I wish there was a way to remunerate.
For her, in my heart I will remain intimate.
She's still part of me not just something I ate!

The Story of Dance

How is it you can get a woman's life story
   in just one dance?
Too much talk about life and romance.
The music is there for us to share.
You have to figure it out from there.
I don't really know what's the right move.
It all depends on the band's main groove.
Just because we're holding hands on the floor,
Doesn't mean there's going to be anything more.
But if there is, "Oh flatter me,"
in my heart so shall you be.
Friends are good, we all need some more.
I'm here for you down on this floor.
There is no reason for you to doubt,
   what you're really all about.
And that's just plain beautiful!

The Shine From Your Smile

The shine from your smile sends me to the moon.
Brighter than a sunlit silver spoon.
All the clocks read midnight, I swear it's noon.
The sound of your voice takes me out of my gloom.
Like listening to music in my very own room.
Sweeps me up like symphonic broom.
Even though I'm not holding your hand,
I can feel your touch from across this land.
Smiling, talking and walking in my rock'n'roll band.
Knowing my body's not up against yours.
I still feel your presence from distant shores.
To hold you again I'd climb five hundred floors.
You are the only woman this man true-heartedly adores.
I know you're not here for my eyes to see.
But in my heart you will forever be.
I keep crying out like a love-sick loon.
Because I can't see your smile from the dark side of the moon.

From My Eyes to My Chin

I have salt stains that run from my eyes to my chin.
They'll soon be washed away, when the tears begin.
Rinse and repeat again and again.
It comes from a well deep within.
Losing my affinity has left my light burning dim.
The martyrdom has left me feeling languorous and grim.
It's a satiety of incessant chagrin.
Is this an arcane or a nightmare's whim?
Getting to the point where I just can't win?
Now the salt stains run down past my chin.

Wasn't Built to be Broken

I thought today was going to be okay
But it ended up being like every other day
I just can't get you out of my mind.
There's no peace in my soul that I can find
It's an endless flood of fears and woe
Hasn't stopped since you had to go.
Every time I think I got it together.
It sneaks up on me like really bad weather
My love for you wasn't built to be broken
More than any words that were ever spoken
To express myself now these words I must use,
In loving you I was not prepared to lose.
The tears out-number the days that pass by
Raining inside even under a blue sky.
Laughter and life can help umbrella the pain.
Eventually the buildup is too much for the drain.
I don't know how long I can swim in this flood.
Starting to get weaker it's thick as mud
I did not give my heart to you as a token
My love for you wasn't built to be broken.

Maybe you can't get over a truly broken heart, but you can find a way to live with it
The way it is "Broken."

To Stop Loving You

I've let myself go because I lost you.
That's something I never thought I could do.
Now I realize what it is that I lack.
It's me not you that I have to get back.
To continue to worship someone that doesn't back at you.
There's not much more damage to yourself you can do.
I guess I can stop stabbing myself in the heart.
Because part of me died anyway, that day you did part.
Now I live in the dark without you around.
In the bottom of the pile in the lost and found.
I know what it is I have to do.
I'm just too afraid to stop loving you.

Today or Tomorrow

I never really learned how to let love go.
It's not something that I wanted to know.
I don't think I can let go all the way.
Just taking it day by day
It's been a living hell, this I will say
To not be here, any price I would pay
My love will never completely fade away
Don't' know if I can do this all alone.
If we could just stay in touch by phone.
Then maybe it will help me to be on my own.
Never had to face something that was this hard.
The flames from our love has left my heart charred
Now I know I can never again let down my guard
All over, I must learn to live alone in my yard.
I will never understand why you had to leave
This will be something I will always grieve
There's another time for us, I truly believe.
Love you too much not to forgive.
Maybe this or another life, together we can live.
Today or *tomorrow*, to you everything I would give

P. S. A call would be great!
    Please don't hesitate!

Tough Lesson

The love of my life has left me in the dust.
My heart to no one now I can trust.
That's all that's left for me is loneliness and lust.
Everything you put into love and it turns out a bust.
There's a lesson to be learned here I know I must.
I guess I was blind about what I now can see.
Just because you are doing something doesn't mean it was
    meant to be.

The Agenda

The agenda of the woman I love
   doesn't include me anymore.
It hurts me deep down into my core.
Now I'm forced to explore
   where I've rarely gone before.
It's so hard to imagine
   there is someone else to adore.
Maybe somewhere out on the dance floor.
Life is not the same
   since she walked out my door.
We should all be making love, not war.
If not for each other, what are we here for?
Living without her has been quite a choir.
Don't know if there's another girl
   that can make my soul soar.
Maybe somewhere out on that dance floor.

As my words of disparity come to an end.
I'm speaking to you as a friend.
My soul goes into this message I send.
Be careful to whom your heart you lend.

                        And that's why

                    Grampo is so

                                        S

                                              A

                                                  D

Now you know what divorce can and will do to people. So I think you should drop everything you're doing and go right to your loved one and hug them as hard and for as long as you can.

Don't wait a minute longer. It does make a difference!

"A picture is worth more than a thousand words…"

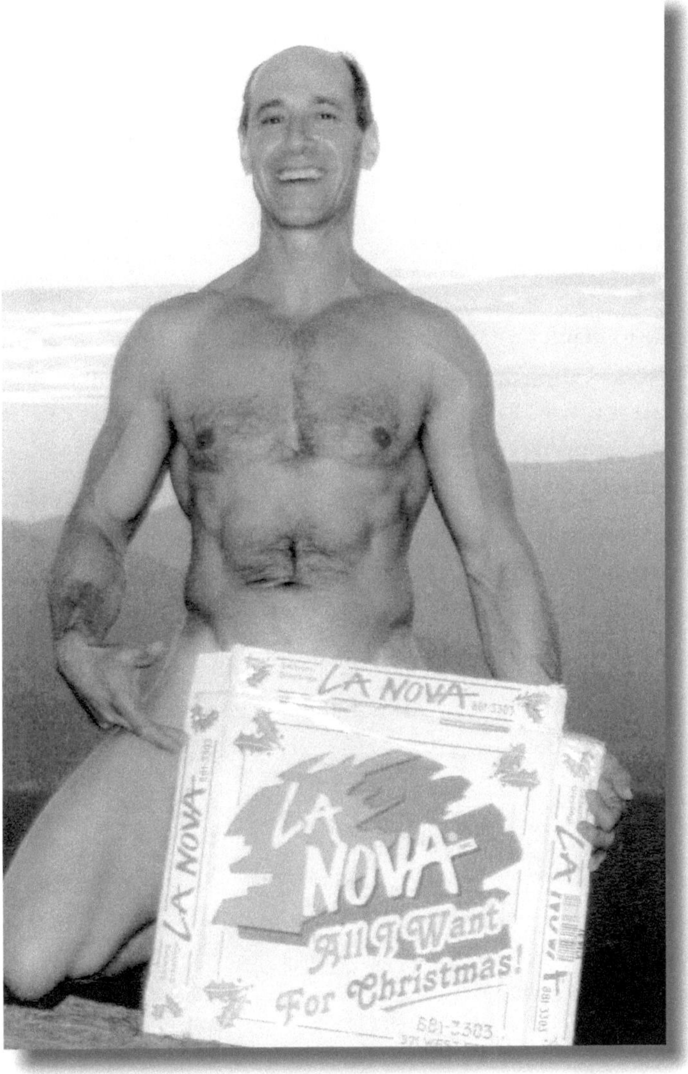
LA NOVA
881-3303
LA NOVA
All I Want
For Christmas!
881-3303

I would like to thank my family and friends, for not talking to me or bringing up the subject of my sadness. This allowed me to work this out in the words by myself. It was hard to get through without a shoulder to cry on. Besides, they all have happy lives with love and security. I didn't want to burden them with my sorrow.

I relied on strangers and professionals to help me through this process. I will be forever in debt to them and consider them my new friends. I hope I can help them someday.

If I could save one relationship with my words that would be great but...

Still, to this day, I would burn 90% of these pages from my heart and soul "not to have lived them!"

Acknowledgments

Thank you to Jill Bobrow for encouraging advice and her special reference.

Special thanks and my utmost gratitude to Kitty Werner (my literary angel) for whom without, this project would be still on my desk. Nobody could have done me one better.

Also, thanks to Judy Benningson (fellow writer) for her critique and words of encouragement.

To the people of the Zen Barn (Waterbury Center, Vermont) thanks for putting up with me and making me feel like I have new friends (which we all need).

A very special thanks to Elijah for his artistry which truly represents my words and inner feelings on this troubling subject which seems to be all around these days. He being a fellow Dead Head was key.

I want to thank Sarah and Mariah from Staples for all their help in providing me this avenue of expression.

I would also like to thank LANOVA Pizza and the Todaro family for providing me with the proper attire and the best pizza in the world.

And anyone who's listening

"Try and stay together"

Harold Boreanaz

www.ingramcontent.com/pod-product-compliance
Lightning Source LLC
Chambersburg PA
CBHW060459080526
44584CB00015B/1489